ME & ARLO

Thank You
for helping me
the other day -
The Book I needed
was at my daughters
AFTER going thru
those pages !
Trish

ME & ARLO

. . .

(it's personal)

TRISH A. LAMPRO

To order additional copies of this title, contact your favorite local bookstore or visit www.tbmbooks.com

Cover and book design by The Troy Book Makers

Printed in the United States of America

The Troy Book Makers
www.thetroybookmakers.com

ISBN: 978-1-935534-0-75

This book is in memory of, and dedicated to, Harold Leventhal, Arlo's business manager and friend, from the New York-based management office.

Harold was a man of integrity and compassion, a man who was loved and respected. I last spoke with Harold in September and he expressed his interest in my book. He was thrilled to be asked to write a forward for me.

Harold passed away before he had a chance to do so.

Harold Leventhal

May 24, 1919–October 4, 2005
Harold, this is for you.

Some of the wonderful people who worked with us on the road have passed.

There was Rocky, one of the best bus drivers.

Dan Velika, bassist. Dan had to be one of the most respected guys and friend to all. He never complained, just went with the flow. And he had such a great sense of humor. How we miss Danny.

Dennis Lachapelle. Another great bus driver. When we were home on our free time, Dennis would do anything for anyone. And he would work long hours for them. No one knew the condition of his heart. It was ticking like a time bomb waiting to go off, and it did, all too soon.

And our wonderful John Pilla.

And of course dear Harold Leventhal.

Me and Ray, the love of my life

ACKNOWLEDGEMENTS

This book is dedicated with love and affection to all the wonderful people I met through my years of working with Arlo Guthrie.

I send warm thoughts and much love to Dear Lou (Dr. Rigali) and Jane Fallon my dearest friend, for forever encouraging me.

To my daughter Kathy, my heart, who's always shown love and support. Your smile and spirit are infectious. I love you for that. You encouraged me and patiently listened. Thank you.

My sons, Chip in Las Vegas and Jimmy and Jody in Washington, who inspire me with their own love of family. I am blessed.

And Ray, the love of my life who stands by me, no matter what I do.

Thank you all—I love you.

November 30, 1983.

I, Jacklyn Guthrie, appoint my secretary, Patricia Iampro, Power of Attorney for all personal and legal matters regarding the Guthrie Family and its Estate.

Jacklyn Guthrie
Beach Road
Washington, Massachusetts

Arlo Guthrie
Beach Road
Washington, Massachusetts

Sworne befoe me this ___30th___ day of November 1983.

Linda R. Kearns
Notary Public

My commission expires February 13, 1987.

This letter is my favorite most prized possession after all the years of gift-giving and gift exchanges. It's a notarized document from the Guthries, giving me power of attorney over the children and their estate. It was my favorite because there was such trust placed in me; for that, I am so honored.

ME & ARLO

OH how the years and your life start out. Quiet, easy and routine. I guess when I look back, mine started out anything but routine.

I was born at home on a Monday afternoon. It started out as any other day. I wasn't due to come into this world on April 12th.

Dr. Haidak, who we affectionately called Dr. Jerry, was dear friends with my parents and made his daily stop on his way home to have a cigarette with my dad and to check on my mother. But dad wasn't home yet.

"Bea," he said, "I'll check you and the baby out." Mom told him she had to go to the bathroom first. Only she didn't have to go to the bathroom, it was me! As soon as she stood up, I slid right out, dropping to the floor. Mom let out a scream and Dr. Jerry came running. As soon as he saw me on the floor, he told Mom to sit down and not touch me. He picked me up, and checked me all over, and after doing everything, to make sure I wasn't injured, he took Mom to the bed making her lie down. After Dr. Jerry examined me again from head to toe, he handed me to mom and went to the kitchen to make her a cup of hot tea. Then he sat down to wait for my dad to come in from work.

Mom and Dr. Jerry were happy I was okay.

This was the year Amelia Earhardt was lost at sea on a round the world flight. The year Germany's pride, "The Hindenberg," exploded in flames over New Jersey. The year the Lincoln Tunnel opened in New York City. And a loaf of bread was .09 cents, a gallon of milk .50 cents, and a new car $760.

All the normal things happened in our lives as we grew up and headed out into the world. I had two brothers, named Rich and "Unk" (for Wayne), and two sisters, named Billie and Jeanne.

Billie had to change "normal" in our family. She was severely burnt in a fire when she was eleven. It burnt the clothes right off her body. She's had two brain tumor operations, and a third one growing. She has Marfan's Disease, and her computer-made shoes cost $500 a pair. She cannot walk at all without them on. She makes no bones about her illness. Billie is a happy person and a wonderful mother who is always "up."

Back then, everyone had a barrel that you burned your papers in. It was Billie's job to put them in the barrel once a week.

As Billie had seen my mother do many times, she thought it was okay to light a match and burn the papers—so she tried it.

But after dropping in the first match, she thought it didn't light; she lit another and set it in just as the first match caught. It flared up and lit Billie's shirt and she was immediately engulfed in flames. Then she did the unthinkable, but because she knew no different, she ran to the house for mom. The clothes burned right off her body and the skin burning with it. She was in such pain, she didn't know what else to do but run for help.

and stay like that for hours. Nothing could be done in any emergency room to correct it, so she'd sit until her arm relaxed, and then it would go back down by itself.

And Billie would smile and say, "Hey, it could be worse."

Billie's children and grandchildren have Marfan's, with tumors that caused loss of sight or the loss of an eye. There were painful back operations where the doctors inserted steel rods to keep the kid's backs straight, because curvature of the spine and tumors are common with Marfan's.

Eventually, Billie and Bob moved to St. Petersburg, Florida to a darling home with fruit trees lining the yard. It was their dream house. The hot weather was another bonus because Billie's bones were very soft, disintegrating, caused by the Marfan's. The bones in her nose were causing her nose to just fall flat on her face. An operation they did, put a plastic insert in to keep the nose in place. Then that insert would ache in the cold weather and harden. So Florida was wonderful.

And then another blow—Bob got leukemia and it took him very fast, and through it all, Billie would say, "God knows what he's doing."

Billie fell in the driveway after Bob died and broke her hip. She lay there until someone driving by saw her and called 9-1-1. They operated on her and sent her home four days later.

She kept falling because her knee hurt so badly and she just could not put any weight on it.

I said, "Billie, have them x-ray it—something's wrong," but they wouldn't listen. I told her to insist: "Go the ER if your doctor refuses to listen. You have insurance." They were so afraid she wouldn't pay.

She went. They finally x-rayed her knee. She had broken the knee at the same time she broke her hip. By now, it's four months later, so rehab was long and painful.

Billie is waiting to have heart surgery for three leaking valves, but she calls herself the "normal" one among us.

AFTER high school, I worked first in a homemade fudge factory, and then later in Sears, Roebuck & Company. I married a wonderful man and had our first son, who we called Chip.

I looked for a place to live. I found an adorable house in Hinsdale. Frannie and I looked at it and we both loved it.

But we had a baby and they said "no" to babies. We told them he was a good baby, very happy, who rarely cried. No—no babies.

So they rented it to an elderly couple who were found dead in the apartment two days later—from carbon monoxide poisoning.

We ended up at a house in Washington owned by Michael Bohan, an FBI agent from New York City. Michael offered us a rent-free cottage to take care of the place while he was in New York City, to mainly just be around. We welcomed Jimmy, Jody and Kathy there.

As the children grew, we built a house on one end of town and Arlo Guthrie and his bride Jackie moved into a large farmhouse on the other end. His real estate broker, Carl Chiaretto, used to laugh and say that we held the town together.

Arlo's manager John Pilla was a very good friend of my husband's, so he would leave us tickets to Arlo's concerts. We'd go from New York to Connecticut. Then John would take us backstage to see Arlo. I liked Arlo immediately. He

Arlo called us "Bonnie & Clyde"
(with John Pilla)

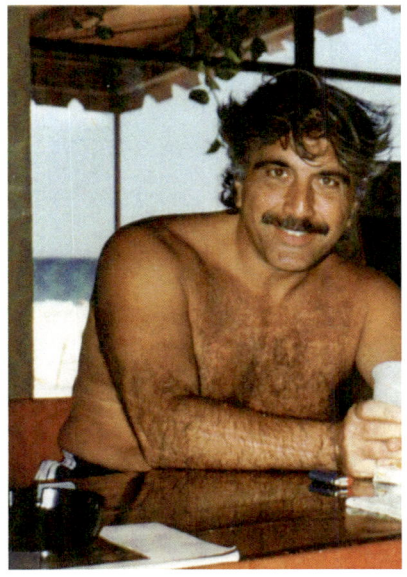

The very handsome John Pilla

was unpretentious and a warm and friendly guy. When Jackie was at a show with him, she too always made you feel welcome. She was fun to be around. Jackie stayed up very late and slept very late. So if you showed up by 2 pm (she might be up), you'd have coffee and talk for a few hours.

Pilla was a big guy who lived year-round in farmer overall jeans. He was without a doubt one of the most handsome guys I ever saw. He'd come by the house, pile the three boys in his car and head to Rhode Island for a day or two at the ocean. They loved to go anywhere with Pilla.

He was a big, gruff guy who had a big, beautiful heart of gold, but it wasn't a healthy heart. John died while awaiting a heart transplant. His life cut far too short. Far too fast.

AROUND the time of John's death I started to drive a school bus. Not the regular big bus but a small van that supposedly went on narrow dirt roads where the big buses couldn't go. No matter what the weather.

There were many times in the spring I didn't think the small van could go either. I got stuck a few times. Even with four wheel drive, the tow truck had to come in after me.

Of course, he'd wait until almost dark, when the spring mud settled down and hardened up a little before he'd venture in after me. So I'd have to sit and wait ... and wait ...

I could never understand why people would build a house four miles in like that. Now that I'm retired, I love the idea. Because now in the winter, you had not only the ice—but a lot of snow to deal with. About this time little Abe Guthrie was going to start kindergarten and it was on my route, so I was due to drive up the hill, a very steep and narrow hill, and yet another dirt road, to pick him up.

All kindergarten children get picked up at their door and brought to school. Only Karl Winters, the boss of the bus transit company, said I was not to drive up to Arlo's house to get Abe. "Let them bring him down to the bottom of the hill if they want him to ride the bus. I'm not letting my bus get stuck up there."

"Karl," I'd argue, "it's the law, he has to be picked up at home. Let me just drive there and get him, Karl, please."

Karl would snap, "You get stuck, you get yourself out."

Well, I didn't care. The boy had the same rights as the others. I was going after him. I knew I was a good driver and if I got stuck, ole' Karl would give in and come and get me.

Boy, was I wrong! I didn't get stuck going after Abe, but I did on a paved road.

I was waiting for a little boy to come out of his house. I pulled over as I was instructed. But because of heavy rain the night before, the road gave way—pavement and all. One side of the van sank right down and I couldn't move.

I called Karl from the walkie-talkie, only to be told "I'll get there when I can. Why did you get stuck?"

Why did I get stuck!?

He got there two hours later. And he had all the other drivers with him. Valada Locke, Marilyn Delaney and Anita Shartrand were brought along to show them this is not how you drive. Like it was my fault the road gave way. Boy, did we have a lot of fun mocking Karl—of course we did this when we were alone! We would all use his strong German accent and talk about the bus getting stuck. Whatever went wrong with those busses, Karl would blame the driver; it was always the driver's fault.

One day as I picked up Abe, he wanted to know if he could come to my house after school and make cookies. "Of course," I said, "but let's ask your mother first."

It was okay with Jackie. So Abe and I set off on the first of many adventures. We made cookies, and then brownies. We also made gifts for his Mom, little cards that Abe hand-drew.

This became a weekly event. After awhile, his little sister Cathy wanted to be there with us, making cookies. Then Annie as little as she was, did not want to be left out so now the four of us were baking once a week.

Arlo was due to head out on tour and wanted Jackie to go along. But there was the matter of the children. Jackie asked if I'd stay at their place and babysit. Yes, as long as I could bring my Kathy. The kids were very excited and we all settled in for a week. We did just fine and it became a regular "sleepover" for me, as the kids called it.

A few days after Arlo and Jackie got back, they both came to see me. "How would you like to come and work for me and get my office straightened out?" Arlo asked, adding "I know you can't just drop the bus run until you get a replacement, so come over whenever you can work around the bus schedule."

I thought I could go 9 to 2. I would get home at 2:15pm, wake up my husband for work, make his lunch and his coffee and head out for the afternoon bus run. By the time my kids got home from school, I had finished my run and we were all home at the same time. My husband worked 4pm until midnight so this schedule worked well for all of us. This went on for a year when Arlo came to me. "Trish, why don't you give up the bus and come up here full-time? There's a lot we'd like to do and we want to include you. It would make it a lot easier than finding a replacement every time we want to take you with us."

I certainly was getting tired of all the nasty back road trips so I agreed to this immediately. Arlo said, "You need a title. How about My personal secretary? Let's get cards made up!"

"Now," he added, "Get your passport. We're going to Germany. You, Jackie and I."

How exciting! We were going to Germany for a concert. We drove to New York City to Arlo's sister Nora's house. We were going to leave the car at Nora and Ted's. They would drive us to the Lufthansa gate. We loaded our luggage and we were on our way. After a long flight of seven hours, we arrived at the hotel for check in. It was a beautiful hotel with fresh fruit baskets for each room and a fully-stocked bar. Everyone was wonderful to us.

Me in Germany

The bodyguard who met us was named Klaus. He took our room numbers and told us he would meet us later to show us around. Germany was very beautiful and very clean. There's no junk and no debris anywhere.

At three in the afternoon, Arlo and I headed out to check out the venue for the following night. I was in the back seat. Arlo was in the passenger seat while Klaus drove.

As we drove down the Autobahn, you could see that the fuel gauge was very low. I knew it was impolite to tell Klaus we were so low, at the same time, remembering I'd heard, il-

Arlo with Sarah and the bodyguard Klaus

legal to run out of gas on the Autobahn. But I kept my mouth shut. He was German. He would know the law.

Sure enough, the car sucked up its last drops of fuel and we coasted to the side of the road—out of gas. One hundred feet down the road was a little house with a family sitting on the front porch. The three of us got out of the car and walked to the house. Arlo had his guitar slung over his back. We asked if there was a gas station anywhere nearby that we could get to. The man on the porch recognized Arlo and told him they had some gas in a can and they would siphon the rest from their car.

Klaus took the gas can back to the car. The family invited Arlo and me to sit down on the porch stoop, so Arlo began to play his guitar a little. The old guy went inside and got his fiddle. They played and sang for nearly two hours! They were so pleased and happy and Arlo was thankful. And poor Klaus, he felt very bad about not checking the gas before we left.

We got back to the hotel around one a.m. and the next day we were out early to shop. We met up with Donovan, and hit all the gift shops before heading for sound check. We did the show with everyone singing right along to all Arlo's songs. They had a wonderful time and so did we.

The next day, they had a big festival in the Hotel de Ville in Rothenburg. The costumed horsemen rode their horses through the streets and some rode right into the hotels, giving rolls, candy and beads to everyone.

When I saw Jackie later I talked about the fun we had and asked, "Wasn't it something the way they rode the horses right into our hotel?"

Jackie said "What! Who rode a horse into the hotel? I never heard a thing!"

Arlo doing the show in Germany

Me in Germany

The last night that we were there and had to start packing to go home, Arlo and Jackie decided to stay for another week or so. I couldn't stay so they thought it would be fun to have me send the kids over. I was going home the next morning on an early flight. Klaus was to pick me up and drive me to the airport. I had my breakfast, my bag was packed and I waited in the lobby for Klaus. He overslept and was full of apologies when he rushed in to the hotel. Poor Klaus! He seemed always to be apologizing.

We drove off to the airport. I was shocked to see the airport full of soldiers with guns patrolling the corridors. I was taken into a cubicle and searched by a female guard, then taken by motor cart right out to the runway where they were waiting for me to board. They took me to my seat, strapped me in, and we were airborne.

I sat next to a nice young man and tried to start a conversation. He looked at me, smiled and said something I didn't understand. He only spoke German. Okay—so for eight hours, I had no one to talk to. I looked in the seat pocket for a magazine. They were all written in German.

Finally, we landed in New York City. Arlo told me to take a cab to Nora's, and Ted would show me how to get on the right road and the best way out of the city.

When the cab driver dropped me off at Nora's house, it was dark. I hung around for a while. I looked in the mailbox for a note. No note. But they didn't know Arlo wouldn't be with me—for him to stay in Germany was a last-minute decision, with no time for a phone call.

Well, I guess I'm doing this trip on my own. And I did. When I finally saw the "Massachusetts Welcomes You" sign, I could have jumped up and down. I was so relieved I could have cried. I'm here, Massachusetts!

Now that I'm home I have to start preparing the kids for Germany. The Guthries decided since I couldn't stay, I would pack up the children and send them to Germany. The kids were adorable. They were so happy to see me. With their parents away, Sarah and Annie clung to me with all their might. I would stay with them. I explained then I would get plane tickets and send them to their parents.

First I had to work on their passports. That would take a full ten days unless I drove to Boston with their photos and did all the paperwork right there. I would then come home with passports in hand. So I got a babysitter and my friend Marilyn and I traveled to Boston City Hall. Things went very smoothly. We had lunch in the courtyard, before going back to Arlo's farm and to see the children.

We drove the two hours back and the children were so happy to see me. Little ones think everybody deserts them when you all go away, even for a day.

I brought them to my house and my daughter Kathy and I tucked them into bed. Annie and Sarah wanted to sleep in Kathy's room. All three were sleeping on air mattresses. All Sarah wanted to know was—how many 'sleeps' until they would see Mommy & Dad? Young Cathy wanted the bed, and Abe? He didn't care where he went.

And it all went well. The next day, we packed the suitcases, and the following day we were to make the trip back to New York to the airport. Irene, who worked in the New York management office for Arlo, booked the flights for me.

I was not looking forward to the trip to New York, so I got my aunt to ride with me one, for the company back and two, to watch the road signs.

The kids were excited they were going to see their Mom and Dad and chatted all the way to New York. We were very early because I was so afraid of getting lost and missing the flight. I couldn't imagine going through all of this and then missing the flight!

We decided to have lunch in the airport and then go to our gate and wait for the flight attendant who would be with the children for the entire trip. The children talked and laughed about the trip. They ran around and played.

And then the flight attendant was there. The kids were still happy and talking a mile a minute when the attendant took Sarah's hand to lead her to the aircraft. Sarah screamed and cried, refusing to go. I walked as far as I could go with them, telling Sarah she would be with her mommy soon. "No, no" she kept crying. There was no turning back. It was flight time.

Sarah didn't care. She wasn't going with this lady she didn't know. She just kept crying, "Trishy, Trishy." Of course, Abe didn't care and Annie was dead silent. Cathy just stared at me.

Poor Sarah ... but they just dragged her along and finally they were aboard.

I cried all the way out of the airport. That little girl trusted me and I just turned her over to a complete stranger. I vowed never to do that to Sarah again.

WHEN the Guthries got back from Germany, Arlo decided to become a Catholic and to follow that religion. So now he wanted to have the children baptized all at once. Jackie and Arlo asked if I would be their Godmother—to all four of them. Of course, I would love it.

On Saturday afternoon, we all met at the church in Hinsdale with Father LeVay offering the prayers of the baptism.

The children were now my Godchildren. And George Laye, who also worked for Arlo, became their Godfather.

George went on to handle The Guthrie Center in Housatonic. We all affectionately called him, "George of Washington."

After the baptisms, we went back to the house and had a luncheon. John Pilla took pictures and Arlo played the piano. Abe climbed right up at one end of the piano, "playing" along with his dad.

THERE was always music in my life when I was growing up. My grandmother played the harmonica. I remember spending every other weekend at her house. She would play that harmonica for hours. It was wonderful.

My mother was a very big square dance caller and traveled all around New York, Connecticut and the New England area. She also could yodel better than anyone. But her career ended when a young man grabbed her by the hand and swung her onto the dance floor—and then let her go.

Mom went flying across the cement floor and crashed into a table, which broke her spine. Mom recovered enough to take care of the family and the house, but her days of entertaining were over.

My son Chip, a surveying engineer in Law Vegas, has played in bands for many years and is a sought-after, excellent lead guitarist. Jody, a master plumber playing in Arlo's band, went on a European tour with him. John Pilla said, if you go on this trip, Jode, I'll give you my guitar when you come back. Jody's boys—Dylan and Dalton—are both talented musicians, just like their dad, playing lead guitar, bass and drums.

Kathy is a graphic designer who occasionally sings with different musicians and enjoys recording studio work as a backup singer. Her husband Peter Adams is one of the best pedal steel players around. And their little guy Jimmy Stet, at 2 years old, has a guitar or piano in his hands all the time. He walks around singing his little heart out!

Following in Dad Pete Adams' footsteps—Jimmy Stet at 2 years old

THE following week, Arlo was going back out on tour. Jackie asked if I could stay. She'd like to go with Arlo for a week before the weather turned bad and before the Christmas holidays. Of course I would stay. My Kathy came over and we all had lots to do together. My boys were older and liked to hang out with their dad!

The fourth night, I put the kids to bed, straightened up, then decided at 9:30pm it was bedtime for me too. As I lay down, I felt content knowing the household was tucked in and cozy. I was awakened by an unfamiliar noise. I sat up and listened, but couldn't make out what was going on. So I got up quickly and pulled on my robe. I went quietly into the hall, making my way from room to room checking in on the children.

As I walked into Annie's room, I stopped dead in my tracks. The light from the window revealed a silhouette of a huge black form bent over Annie's bed. This person was repeating over and over to a sleeping Annie, "Where's your dad? Tell me where your dad is! Where is he?"

I was petrified. I tried to sound calm as I said, "Hello? What can I do for you? Come out in the kitchen where we can talk!"

She kept saying the same thing to Annie, who thank God did not wake up.

"Come on now," I repeated, "Let's go in the kitchen. Come on now."

Finally, she stood up straight and she scared me all the more. She was huge. She was dressed all in black with very long, straight black hair. She must have been 5'8" and 200 pounds. She came toward me and started to smile. I backed into the kitchen, not wanting to turn away from her. The woman was coming right at me.

When we got into the lighted area, I saw that her slacks were split all the way down the outside seam. I stood right near the door, and asked what she was doing in the house. Why she took it upon herself to walk right in without permission.

I asked her over and over again, what did she want? And how did she even get in? Her not answering made me turn furious and terrified, at the same time.

I kept questioning, repeating myself, and she finally replied that she had hitch-hiked from New York state. She further offered, unbelievably, that she had stayed in the barn until all the lights were out in the house. I was getting worried over her reluctance to leave.

I glanced up at the clock. It was 11:30 pm, and I couldn't reach the phone. I opened the door to the enclosed porch and slowly talked her into going outside. She argued that she couldn't leave. She flatly refused, saying that she had nowhere to go.

I spoke in even tones. "You came all the way from New York State. Now go back."

"No," she challenged me, "I can't leave. What am I supposed to do? I can't go anywhere." I just stared, scared to death of this woman.

Another moment passed in silence. Finally—just like that—she turned and left through the open door. I rushed to lock it behind her and ran to the phone. I called the state police and was told that as soon as the roads were clear, they would be over to check things out. I scrambled over to the switch for the outside floodlights. When I threw on the switch, I just couldn't believe it. There must have been three feet of swirling snow!

I went to all the windows. There wasn't a trace of her anywhere. Now I felt guilty: Where was she? After I locked everything—and left the flood lights blazing all around the house—I went around and gathered up all the sleeping children. I took the four Guthrie children and my daughter and I put them into bed with me. I never slept that night.

The next morning after the plow came through, Charlotte Morgan—the only other one to live on Beach Road—came up to see me. "You won't believe what happened at my farm last night," she said. Charlotte, who heats her house with wood, told me she got up at 2 in the morning to feed the stove. And when she walked in the kitchen, there sitting at the table was the mysterious woman in black! Charlotte had laced right into her, giving her hell for walking into her home like that. She ran her farm alone, and was the hardest worker I ever met.

She had been aware of the snow outside and had informed the woman that she could stay in the house until 6 in the morning. Then Charlotte was going to drive her to the bus station to take a one-way trip to Albany. And she was never to come back.

Well, she never did come back. But she called and she sent things. She was persistent, this girl. Then as surprisingly as she appeared that night, she disappeared.

WORKING at the Guthrie's had a very big bonus for me. I met a girl who was to become, and remain, one of my truest friends. Jane Fallon was Jackie's housekeeper, and we hit it off right away. Jane was doing side jobs so she could put herself through nursing school. She went on to become a very compassionate and caring registered nurse. But in the meantime, we became best friends and had more fun working than I ever dreamed possible at a job.

The Guthries loved Jane. And trusted her judgment with their house. They loved it when we would change things around while they were gone. Be it painting or changing furniture around, they loved it. Jane always came up with great ideas. I didn't have a lot to do when Arlo was away, so I joined right in working alongside Jane.

"Let's bring this dresser upstairs," Jane would announce, "It will be something different."

We'd get it half way up the stairs and I'd yell "Wait a minute, hold it, Jane!" and she would. I ran to get my camera. What a great shot that will make. All the while, Jane's hanging on to the dresser.

One day, we painted the cellar stairs from the top to the bottom. Now, we're at the bottom with nowhere to go until the stairs dried!

Jane got the brilliant idea to sand the hard wood floors— and it did seem like a good idea. So after we finished sanding the floors, because they looked so beautiful, she thought it would be great to do the chop block in the middle of the floor.

I told her the dust would ruin the work we already did. "No," Jane countered, "I have the greatest plan. You hold the sheet over the chop block and I'll run the sander." So that's what we did.

Until the sheet got caught in the sander and rolled right up in and the sander quit, screeching to a halt. Jane was right—the dust stayed right under the sheet. All over us.

But when we got through, it was beautiful. Arlo and Jackie loved how they looked. They said with a laugh that they should go away more often! Jane agreed. Because there was some painting she wanted to do in the kitchen. Since the floors looked so nice, she thought the walls should be freshened up, too. Fresh paint—that's what was needed!

So when Arlo went on his next trip, we encouraged Jackie to go along. Jane got a gallon of paint, a nice soft creamy color. She set up the stepladder and, leaning over the refrigerator, started painting the wall.

Now, Jane hates mice and is totally frightened at the mere mention of a mouse. What happens of course? Along comes a mouse. It was a little baby mouse who jumped off the refrigerator right onto her shoulder, and then jumped down onto the floor.

Jane's screams could be heard a block away, I swear. She jumped off the ladder into the gallon of paint, which splashed all over the newly-sanded and finished floor.

I could not stop laughing.

Jane could not stop screaming as the paint splattered on her glasses, with her foot still jammed in the paint can.

She managed to sit down to catch her breath and then glanced at the clock. It was 4 pm and it was Lenten season. Jane went to church with her mother every day during Lent. She jumped up, wiggled her foot out of the paint and off she goes.

I called after her, "Jane! There's paint all over you!"

She didn't care, she was gone. It's church time!

It was never boring at work and you never knew what would happen day to day. One morning when I got there, Arlo wanted to know what my plan was. Would it be a busy day or could I take off with him somewhere? I told him that I had nothing in particular going on, so he said, "Let's go for a ride."

And off we went. Where? To New York City, to buy Jackie a car for her birthday.

It was so hot in the city in mid-summer, that we did what we had to do as quickly as possible. We met with Harold Leventhal in the New York office. We loved it when we could stop in and spend time with Harold. Mr. Class Act himself!

We went from there to the car dealership, then to the bank, and then within two hours, we were on our way home again with the new checker cab Arlo called Kanardly. He drove Kanardly and I was in the big black Monster Cadillac (as he called that one). We stopped for a quick lunch and then headed back to Massachusetts, one following the other.

Jackie was sleeping in when we left and had no idea where we were. As we drove up, now she was standing on the front porch. "Hey Arlo, hi Trish—where have you guys been? Arlo, do you want to go to the movies? It starts in half an hour."

"Sure," he said, "Let's go."

THE next day, Arlo wanted me to take the day off. Because it was a Friday, I decided to go to Chicopee to the Folk Festival put on by two of Arlo's biggest fans, Charlene and Jim Murphy. I was ten minutes into the trip and as I headed down Route 8, a black bear weighing roughly 250 pounds jumped over the guardrail right into my Volkswagen Rabbit. Breaking a headlight on the Rabbit and killing the bear outright.

The state police were called. The Town of Becket Chief of Police Bill Robinson was called. I was able to drive my VW Rabbit for two weeks before they could fix it, but Paul Harvey picked up the story and it went across the airwaves as "Rabbit Kills Bear."

Of course, that headline started Jim and Charlene sending every bear joke and gift they could find. There was a bearskin

Arlo and Charlene

Jim & Charlene Murphy

rug, bear feet slippers and shirts with bear cartoons. Charlene has sent me Moose jokes for seventeen years. But that took a break while she found every bear joke around.

Charlene and Jim Murphy have followed Arlo around from concert to concert for years. She had a notebook with every venue that Arlo played in with mileage, travel times, what roads to take to get there, parking information, restaurants to eat in once they got there, and pit stops areas needed along each route. They did all this to assist travel to his concerts. They were, in a word, dedicated. They were among the greatest fans. They did a show on the radio called "Friends and Folk." I told them it should be called "Arlo's Hour" because that's about all they played: Arlo and Pete Seeger. The Murphy's are both schoolteachers and Charlene got her class interested in Arlo's songs. They were teenagers who got involved in every aspect of his music. When they worked hard at a project, Charlene would reward them with a song break.

On State House steps

Left: *On State House steps*
Right: *In Murph's living room—bumper stickers everywhere*

They decided to take their involvement to another level. They felt his song, "Massachusetts" should be our state folk song. And they set out to accomplish just that.

They wrote letters to senators, to representatives and congressmen. They made phone calls and posters. And always kept in touch with our office, making sure they followed all the legal steps.

They had tag sales and food sales to raise money for a bus to drive us all to Boston to the state house. Once we got this step out of the way, we would be going back if it passed in the house. After months of hard work and dedication, they had achieved their goal. They got word it had been accepted. Arlo Guthrie's song "Massachusetts" would be "the official Massachusetts' state folk song."

I am honored and pleased to name those children who made this happen. They are: Mariclare Murphy, Lisa Phillips, Christine Moran, Cynthia Pise, Karen Michalski, Paul Jendrysik, Gail Desrosiers, Cheryl Flynn, Ronald Jendrysik, Christine Pike, Christina Fredette, Angela Montemagne and Rebecca Berthold. Thanks also to State Rep. Kenneth M. Lemanski, D-Chicopee. Thank you Charlene and Jim Murphy for your dedication to this project.

There were more than 600 letters and over 1,444 handmade, silk-screened bumper stickers. House bill #6499 was approved by the senate and signed by Governor Edward J. King on August 5, 1981 at 12 noon. The Guthrie family thanks all of you, each and every one for the hard work and for the love you put into this special project.

Arlo is so honored.

It's wonderful when you can say, "I love my job—I love to go to work." We all have to work and it certainly makes it easier if you can enjoy your daily routine.

I would get to work at nine (the magic hour to go to work) and Arlo and Jackie and I would sit at the table having coffee and discussing our day. We'd get the paperwork out of the way and the interviews and then the afternoon would be free.

Arlo decided one afternoon to drive into town and do a little shopping. He came back a few hours later with his purchase: a parrot named Max. Now Max was a beautiful bird. He was composed of brilliant colors like red, yellow and blue. Max fluttered around his cage that was always left with the door opened. He'd squawk and squawk and try to cause a scene and get attention. And he hated women.

Jane found out the hard way. She was cleaning the cage and as she held one side, her fingers wrapped in the wire and Max came squawking over and bit down on her finger—drawing blood. She blamed herself for getting too close. There was a screen to hold up while you cleaned the bottom of the cage and Jane didn't use it.

The next day while I was in the office, Arlo buzzed me on the intercom: "Trish, come on in, I just finished a new song and I'd like you to hear it." My office was in a building next to the top house. I picked up my notebook in case he had anything for me to jot down and went to the house. I opened the front door and announced, "Here I am." And this set our darling Max—who was perched on the back of the rocking chair—into a tizzied flight and he darted right at me, landing squarely on the side of my head. That of course sent me into a panic and I waved my arms wildly screaming, "Arlo!! Max's got me!" and thus with my waving arms, I knocked Max to the floor.

Arlo picked the bird up and closed him in his cage. Then he got me a glass of water and sat me down on a chair to catch my breath.

Well, that was it for Max. Dear Max was now getting ready for a new home. When we look back on Max's stay, everyone except Arlo was afraid of him.

Along came Dennis. Dennis said he would love to take Max! So Max had his new home and companion. We were all so relieved to see him go. Of course, Jane had to say to Arlo, "Oh I'm so sorry to see Max go. We'll miss him, won't we Arlo?"

R IGHT at this time, Arlo got the idea to move the office down to the bottom house. It was down there when I first came to work. It got moved up to the barn for a year but Jackie wanted to use the barn as a recording studio so we started making plans to put the office back in the bottom house. It was a beautiful house that doubled as guest quarters, a meeting room and an office. It only took a couple of weeks and when we finished it was very functional and efficient with a lot of windows and a great deal of sunlight.

Once in a while, even in the office, you would run into a problem with a fan. One problem I had was from a nurse at Berkshire Medical Center. She left notes. She'd call. One day as I sat in the office, she came right up to the house in her yellow VW and opened the car door and called out to Arlo's dog. He hopped right in the car with her, but as soon as she drove off, the dog started acting up so bad she had to stop and let him out. Then two days after that, I found a note on my desk from this woman that said if she couldn't have Arlo, she'd get to Jackie! I went right up the hill to talk to Arlo about the problem with this woman, but he had already taken Jackie to town. A further shock was that when I went back to the office, the note was gone. I started locking the door to the bottom house, never telling anyone why, because the note was gone and I had no proof the woman had even done these things. I wanted us to be safe. Had she been in the house the whole time? I didn't even know.

When I started locking up, she just disappeared. And that was the end of her! The only other time I had any trouble with a fan was when I became road manager. It was in Gaithersburg, Maryland. It was a big fair and during the sound check. A man sitting with his family in the bleachers had a movie camera and was filming the sound check.

Arlo said to me, "There's no copyright on this song yet. Have him stop."

I went to the man and told him he could not film. Please stop. But he wouldn't stop. The fact that he did not want to stop was irrelevant. He must stop. I stood in front of him. No luck. He wouldn't stop.

A man behind him stepped forward and announced "I'm with the state police, is there a problem here?" But the filming man refused to look at him or stop even then. This went on and the cop made no more headway than me. This guy was going to film this event.

So we did one thing the guy did not plan on. We stopped Arlo. The man calmly shut off the camera, took his family and left. I never saw him again. I watched and waited. He never came back for the concert.

I had to meet Noel in his trailer to settle the financial end of the show. As soon as the band went on stage, I headed for the trailer. Noel met me at the door and we went inside to count money. He pulled out a big paper bag that he handed to me, and said "Trish, start counting, I forgot something."

So I opened the bag and had counted out the $15,000 before Noel returned. He returned with a small paper bag. "Everything's there," he said, "oh, except this."

He handed me the bag. "Open it, open it," he urged. Inside was a little hand-blown lollipop pin he had a glass blower at the fair make for me. It was so beautiful and special. We hugged, signed the necessary paperwork and then Noel said, "Put that money in a safe place and come with me."

So I took off my cowboy boots, put several thousand in each boot, put my boots back on and we were off. Noel took me to a shirt maker at one of the booths. The man who ran the booth wanted to give me and Arlo one of his beautiful handmade shirts. I still have my shirt and the little lollipop pin from Noel.

ABOUT this time I was getting calls in the office from Florida. They wanted Arlo to go to West Palm Beach and do some commercials for a Save the Turtles campaign. Turtles are being destroyed at an alarming rate. There were cans of turtle soup in the markets and in local restaurants. They were being run over by boats and used as bait for large fish. They are being exploited by man for oil, leather and food. Some turtles can net as much as 200 pounds of meat. Calipee, which is a yellow gristle-like material, is an indispensable ingredient for turtle soup recipes. There are rough-

Hollywood Bob & Arlo

ly 250 kinds of turtles and no matter what their habitat is, all turtles lay their eggs on land.

Turtle families—there are seven families of turtles: soft shell turtles, snapping turtles, musk and mud turtles, land tortoises, freshwater turtles, sea turtles and leatherback turtles.

So after some research, Arlo thought it would be a worthy cause to do whatever he could, including a concert to raise money for the turtle tanks and care for babies or injured turtles. We made the necessary arrangements to go to West Palm Beach.

Arlo digging turtle eggs after getting permit

We stayed for a week at the marina, and then we were moved to the Colonnaide Hotel where we were granted carte blanche.

When Arlo and I arrived at the hotel, Ron had his secretary take me on a tour. The top floor of the hotel, the entire fifth floor, was the Bob Hope Suite. It was spectacular. An eight-foot wide staircase winding its way up from the forth floor led into a foyer as big as a living room. There was a poolroom and three living room areas. It was very spacious and open.

The view was perfect. Actually, everything about the place seemed perfect. The kitchen alone was every woman's dream kitchen. Then the secretary took my picture and put it in a casing that read "The Bob Hope Suite." It was a ready-made key chain. I kept it for years afterwards, until it faded and wore out.

While we were in West Palm Beach, we did everything from Florida's massive flea markets to taking boat rides. The girls took me to luncheons and to baby showers. It was beau-

Arlo interviewing as the roving turtle beach reporter

tiful staying at the Colonnaides Hotel. It was the biggest hotel at the time in the area.

The plans were made to do commercials for public awareness. We would do one commercial at the ocean every day. Then go to the television studio at night. We'd do editing, reviewing, then put it on the air the next day. We would do this for a week. When we went to the ocean to dig up turtle eggs, we had a waiting period. Arlo had to have a license to even touch the eggs and that license took two days. You also must have a legitimate reason. We had nothing to do until 3pm when Arlo would film again. So digging for eggs for the hatchery would have to wait.

Arlo said, "Let's go to the beach," which was right out the door at the back of the hotel. He said that I should go in the water to get the salt water in my hair. Come on. So we ran into the water. We were just to our knees. And all of a sudden we found ourselves in water up to our neck. One wave after another kept pounding over us. The waves kept sending us out farther and farther.

I can swim—but just barely. I was getting very frightened. Arlo kept his cool and said to take hold of his hand, we'd get back to shore and all would be okay. We discovered that was not going to work, because we were oily and kept slipping away.

It was time to make a decision. Arlo announced that he was going to have to go for help. He said he'd get a lifeguard with a towrope for me. And as he swam away and back to the shore, he said something, which—even in the middle of this horrific situation—was ironically funny. He said, "Don't go away. I'll be right back."

I'd never been so frightened in my entire life. I glanced at the shore, but it looked so far away. The waves kept crashing on me and I turned to see when the next one was going to hit. Actually, that movement—turning to look—is what saved my life.

Just as I turned, a wave would hit me and send me sideways with incredible force. It was such a strong force that I was sure I would not survive it. I felt like a rag doll twisting and turning in what seemed like an eternity, waiting for help to arrive. Eventually, I landed on a sandbar, with the water just rolling over the tops of my feet.

I got my bearings, and I looked up and called "Arlo, help!"

At the same time that the wave hit me, Arlo reached shore. He ran to the lifeguard stand, calling for somebody to help. But there wasn't anybody there. A sign on the side of the guard stand said: "GONE TO LUNCH." Arlo turned away and knew he had to go back after me himself. He was pretty exhausted. As he started to run back to the ocean, he looked up and stopped. He didn't see me, he later reported.

"Oh my God," he thought, "she's drowned. What do I do? I have got to tell her family that she's drowned." He said he was devastated and shocked at the thought but then he heard my voice calling from the sandbar. He came to me and brought me to the blanket.

What was so amazing to me was all the sunbathers on the beach who just watched everything and not one went to get some help or offered to help in any way!

Making sure I was all right, Arlo went to get the girls from the marina to take care of me. They were all involved in the turtle project. They were the ones who would take care of the eggs and the hatchlings.

It was time for the next commercial spot and we were trying to keep a tight schedule. Assured I was okay, just badly shaken, Arlo left as soon as the girl got there.

We sat for a while so I could relax. Then we went in the hotel. I took a long, hot shower. We all had dinner together and then left for a lecture with Ross Witham who was the guest speaker. Ross is the author of "Turtles: Extinction or Survival?"

I have no idea how I sat through the lecture. As interesting as it was, I could not wait for it to end. I felt like I had 100 pounds sitting on top of my head! I had to lie down, as soon as possible. I just didn't feel good.

We were now expected at the TV station to review the film from the day before. I had to beg off, so the girls drove me back and after another long hot shower, they put me to bed.

I lay in that one spot the whole night. Me, who usually tosses and turns all night long, never moved once.

When morning came, I felt fine. I was up and ready to roll with the rest of them. This should have been a warning sign to go to a doctor!

After another shower, as hot as I could stand, I finished dressing just as the girls came to the door. Jamie, Cathy and Vicki came in with toast, eggs and bacon. There was also hot coffee and watermelon. We headed for the beach. They wanted me to go in the water, but I refused. No way. What if I get caught in the waves again? They said that I could not get caught in the waves again. The water was as calm as a bathtub.

I know, so you know how stupid I'll look screaming in a calm ocean? No way, not me! I had terrible nightmares for years about the ocean. I was being flipped through the water over and over again in these bad dreams.

Ron E. Kairella, as he always introduced himself, had a big party for us as the work on the turtle project came to an end. He hired a band and invited everybody. They were all a close-knit group and they were very loyal. Ron gave Arlo and his family an open invitation to take vacations anytime they

Go back in that ocean! Don't be afraid

wanted at the hotel, and for as long as they wanted to stay. He also extended the same to my family and I.

A few days later, we finished up with the project. It had gone very well and we were all pleased. We said our good-byes and gave our hugs to everyone and then we left for the airport. And in the following year when I went for a week's getaway, Ron gave me keys to the 'suite.' "Stay and enjoy," he said." I had an open invite to the dining room for all my meals. And because he was the honorary owner, he could do as he pleased. So I stayed in the Bob Hope Suite for one week (And I honestly didn't think Bob Hope went down to visit anymore.)

Everything went along well and we enjoyed it all, although we did not abuse the privilege or overstay our welcome. Ron would sit with us at night in the dining room bar area, having a great time himself. He never seemed to slow down.

Arlo's note to me

And then two years later, the power—which was known to go out on Singer Island because of tropical storms—went out. Ron E. Kairella ran up the stairwell to the fourth floor. That's where the elevator always seemed to get stuck when the power outages happened. Ron wanted to make sure no one was trapped inside the elevator.

He pressed the elevator button several times and pushed on the door, the door opened with such force that as he leaned into the opening just ever so slightly, it sucked him right in and he fell to the bottom. He fell to the basement. Five floors down.

Ron E. Kairella was dead. The whole island was devastated. He was the life force of that island and he left behind his wife Carol and their four children, his brother Sammy and many devoted friends. A year went by and they closed the hotel. Then another year went by and they tore it down. The island was never the same.

During that wonderful time we knew Ron and stayed at his hotel, we knew we benefited from his great kindness and gracious qualities as a host and will always hold those years in fond memory.

After our extended stay, helping promote turtle safety for public awareness, we flew back to New York City. We went to the New York office, and then to Arlo's mother, Marjorie Guthrie's apartment near Central Park. Marjorie, Arlo and I went to an early dinner before we would head back to Massachusetts. Arlo said, "Trish, tell my mother what happened to you in Florida." So we tell Marjorie the story involving the ocean, and Marjorie said, "My, you should be careful."

As soon as we got to the airport, I knew I wouldn't like this plane ride. It was a small, no—make that very small—plane, that you strapped yourself in, never stood up, held your breath, grabbed someone, and flew to Pittsfield.

The next day, while we had our coffee and discussed the day's events, Arlo told me to look, and he showed me his arm, the imprint from my fingers still visible. So much for flying in those small planes.

![Photograph of a woman seated in a chair on a porch at night]

Me in my days as Arlo's personal secretary

ONE morning Arlo, Jackie and I sat around talking. We'd had a busy few weeks and our policy was then to take it easy for a couple of days. Jackie said, "Let's relax." She always made me feel relaxed—no matter what was going on. She has that gentle nature.

Let me tell you about Arlo's wife, Jackie Guthrie. She is a most gentle and generous person. Always easy-going and giving. Not to mention a gorgeous creature with a smile that could magically light up a room ... and hold it spellbound. She could put together a luncheon for five of the girls or a party for fifty with such ease, that Martha Stewart would take notice. Jackie had a relaxing way about her and she would take anyone under her wing. A wonderful mother, and now a grandmother. Jackie is a breast cancer survivor and has been cancer-free for 10 years.

Doug Dillard came up to the Guthrie's for a visit. He is Mister Fun. Doug and I decided we were going to get ourselves tattoos. He had an elaborate plan for his tattoo and I always wanted a daisy. As it turned out, Doug got a phone call from his manager about a TV interview and he had to leave before we had time to get our tattoos. And it is just as well, because at this stage of my life, the daisy would be a little wilted flower.

NOW, Ramblin' Jack Elliot is on his way, so we're going to just hang out. He'd planned a few days, but we were having so much fun, he stayed a full week and everybody enjoyed every minute. We loved Jack.

Then just as Jack left, Hoyt Axton came in. He was a darling man who died of a massive heart attack. (Hoyt's mother Mae co-wrote Heartbreak Hotel with Elvis Presley.) Hoyt was physically a big, burly man who was just a wonderful old softy at heart. I remember him telling me in that great, baritone voice of his, "Trish. I just love corn puffs." He could eat a big bag for breakfast and not feel the least bit guilty. "I'm just in love with those little things," he said with a smile.

Arlo liked to leave me little notes on my desk or on my windshield of my car. They were fun notes, serious notes and surprising ones. Some were poems when I was sick and one on my birthday was a funny note with a $100 bill attached. If you made a mistake, Arlo never got mad. He'd say, "Let's try that again." And he has the most wonderful sense of humor. Arlo felt you worked with him, not for him.

A RLO was booked to do three shows in Bermuda. It was to be a week of fun in the sun, shopping, dining, sightseeing and just hanging out plus the three concerts.

Jackie hugged me in the office: "Arlo said to make sure your passport is up to date. You're going to Bermuda with us." (I was very excited but all I could think of was The Bermuda Triangle!) It turned out to be a good flight. And we all had a wonderful time.

I remember a special moment at the last show on the island. It was beautiful and touching. We were sitting in a round booth. Arlo was on stage, singing "Hobo's Lullaby." The children were sleeping, draped all around Marjorie, who sat with her eyes closed, humming and gently patting Sarah on her back. Yes, a very moving moment.

Marjorie was a darling woman. Every week there would be an article in the mail from her about food and healthy eating. A former principal dancer with Martha Graham, she was a complete believer of a healthy life style. No junk food, no soda, no smoking or drinking.

She would walk to work, no matter what the weather. She said sometimes she had to hold on to a light post because the wind was so strong. I'd tell her to take a cab, but she said No, walking is so healthy for you.

Marjorie was a tireless worker in originating a committee to assist her drive to find a cure for Huntington's disease, which her husband and Arlo's father Woody Guthrie died from. She passed away at age 65 on March 13, 1983. I believe the following piece about her sums it all up:

A SALUTE TO MARJORIE

When Marjorie Guthrie established the Committee to Combat Huntington's Disease just sixteen years ago, she was filling a personal need to learn about this mysterious disease. While she may have recognized the importance of her future efforts, she could never have realized her impact. How could she have ever known then the thousands of people worldwide who would be better equipped to understand, to cope, to dream of a cure for Huntington's disease?

It has been through Marjorie's dreams, through her ability to see a problem, analyze it and tackle it head on, that CCHD has become a major force among health agencies with national and international recognition. Her energy, her enthusiasm and her spirit will continue to inspire us in our efforts to see that her mission is fulfilled. For through her energy we must find the strength to confront and find a cure for Huntington's disease.

Last fall, Marjorie announced that she would be taking a one-year sabbatical from her work to devote herself to some special projects, one being a comprehensive care center for chronic, neurologic patients at the state-supported Helen Hayes Hospital in Haverstraw, New York.

In a salute to Marjorie Guthrie's work, CCHD has committed $10,000 toward the establishment of the Marjorie and Woody Guthrie Wing, which will include respite care beds in the neurologic center at the Helen Hayes Hospital. As we sorrowfully bid our farewell to Marjorie, we cannot dwell on her untimely death, but must be energized by her spirit, her will and her determination. Those qualities of hers must compel us to continue to work with an urgency like never before.

Robert K. Rusk, President
Committee to Combat Huntington's Disease
On behalf of CCHD's Board of Trustees and Staff

ONE day when I got to the office, Arlo said we had a lot to do. His arms were loaded with paperwork for me. The night before while watching television, Arlo heard some very disturbing news.

I'd had to call senators and congressmen. It was in regards to what we Americans came to call "The Boat People." The program told how women and children were raped, beaten and thrown overboard. Many of the males were loading boats and trying to save entire families.

Arlo had to do something to help. I was on the phone all day imploring that we help save these people. One congress-man after another congressman was called and by the end of the day, they told me that Arlo would have a family to host at his house, as soon as the paperwork was ready.

They were the Van Huynh family: a father, sons, children and two of the wives. We were going to let them stay in the bottom house.

Uh-oh, let's move the office once again. Jackie was to organize a moving crew and then a cleaning bee would happen the following week. As we gathered a group of friends, Jane would be in charge of who worked where. Jane did a wonderful job for she seemed to fit the right person to the right job and soon it all was finished and beautiful. In between the jobs, we all had some laughs and we were excited about what would take place on the farm in just a few more days.

We're ready. We get the call. They will arrive at 6 o'clock. Jackie, and her sister Juanita, who's an absolute darling, stayed in the top house making a homemade soup for the Van Huynh family. Everything is done and then—the Van Huynh family arrives.

The challenge begins. They speak little English. Kim, one of the sons, and Nhueh, the father can speak with us. Everyone laughs. We will get the hang of this. We show them around the house and decide to give them some privacy. They have to be tired.

Jackie and Juanita bring the soup down. And as they walk in the house, there's the family on the stepladder, washing the ceiling light fixtures. Someone else was cleaning the outlet switches on the wall. Checking every detail. They were cleaning and cleaning.

They were very hard working and went right out and got jobs right away. Kim opened a restaurant and did very well. Some of the sons took their families and moved to California. The father went to West Virginia and managed a hotel until his death.

I remember when it was my birthday. It was a Saturday and I had a very busy weekend. They bought me a cake and hunted me down for two days to give me the birthday cake. And they sent me letters.

The young ones would often apologize and say, "You know, we didn't want a war either." And that would grab at your heart. The small children had nightmares and they would cry easily. They would say they had much respect for Arlo.

When they moved on and everyone got their own place, guess what? We moved the office back.

B RUCE Clapper who was the road manager for maybe twelve years with Arlo, decided to retire from the road and stay close to home to watch his son grow. Arlo began to look for a road manager and there I was. Right under his nose. I'd been in the office for ten years and now here I was going on the road with Arlo and his band.

Matt McKeever was one of the nicest guys to be on the road with. He was a joy to have around. He never complained. He was never late. He never asked for anything unreasonable. Matt is now a registered nurse and thankfully is still very

Me—working from home

much involved with making music. After a serious accident he is back and healthy.

And there was Bob. Bob Williams WAS his steel guitar. He could make that steel guitar talk. And he would mesmerize with the elegant way he played.

There were other guys and bus drivers. Lots of bus drivers. Lots of different drivers. (And everybody gets initiated.) My initiation took place like this: I went along while Bruce finished up his last two weeks, showing me the ropes as we went. Bruce was riding shotgun up front with the driver. I was in my seat half way down the bus. I was reading my paperwork and making notes.

All of a sudden, the driver is standing in the doorway and yelled "Hey Trish, would you get me a soda?"

I looked up and screamed "WHAT ARE YOU DOING? Who's driving the bus??"

Work is hard on the road

Everybody roared! Bruce had slipped into the driver's seat at the last red light and they kept the door shut so I couldn't see what they were doing. Okay—they got me!

That year on my birthday, we had to ride over the Golden Gate Bridge as we headed into San Francisco, California. In the distance, you could see the former Alcatraz state prison on the left. Because I hate heights, they made me sit in the front, riding shotgun. And look out the window! I told them I was going to keep my eyes closed until we got to the other side.

No way! This is your birthday present and we'll just stop in the middle of the bridge until you open your eyes and look.

As the driver slowed down, I peeked and Oh my God, decided I better look right now. So they drove on and we were finally over that bridge. When we got across, I said, "Oh thank you, thank you—I loved it!"

And there were nicknames: Moose and B.C. and Dog, Teacher, A.D.G. and Sarah Face. There was Chipanaze and Jiminaze, Frantic Fran (a.k.a. Foster), Kak, Jobi and Abish.

Me with Mackenzie Phillips

THERE are some strange things that happen on stage when you least expect it. A lot of stars like a big, flashy introduction when they go on stage. They want you to go on and on about what they've accomplished, their awards or good deeds and who their best friend of importance is. Arlo is not one of those people. He is very unpretentious. He prefers to just dim the lights and walk on stage. There are a few times you can say, "Arlo Guthrie." The way this venue was laid out, you had to come down a flight of stairs, you then turn left and go up five steps to the stage. But the manager at the club wanted to do the latter.

After a long discussion, he gave me his word not to go on and on about Arlo. He would only introduce "Arlo Guthrie" which would be my cue to get Arlo down the staircase and up the five.

Now it's showtime. The guy is up on stage and waving to the audience as he walks up to the mike. And lo and behold, he goes into a Johnny Carson-type routine, a warm-up monologue. I nearly fainted. Arlo said, "Trish. What's he doin'?!"

I had no idea what he was doing. I had no clue.

Arlo pressed, "Trish, didn't you tell him I don't like an 'intro'?" What's he doin'?? Get him off of there!"

So I walked on stage but he kept on with his routine— and the stuff wasn't even funny. I looked at him and he looked back at me, but kept right on going. So he left me with no choice. I took his arm (if I had a meat hook like on the Gong Show I would have used it) and led him right off of the stage, all the while he's doin' his routine. Later, he confessed to me that he just got carried away. We would laugh about the poor guy later, but it was not the least bit funny at the time.

One of the meals that we had on the road, which I will never forget, was Arlo's request for a "light" dinner. I told the manager of an upcoming venue that Arlo would want a "light" meal. I told him Arlo would want a small tuna fish salad and that would be fine, with fresh coffee and real cream. That was it.

The man in charge of this particular venue was very excited. "Oh!" he said, "I can do a wonderful tuna salad. And I'll have lots of hot, fresh coffee!" (That would be perfect.) And it was just going to be Arlo performing—no band this time. Just a small amount of food was all that was needed.

So Arlo was doing his sound check and I went in the dressing room to check things out. In the middle of a round table sat a tray with a tuna salad that I swear was made with six cafeteria-sized cans of tuna fish. And it was smiling at me! Piled high, it had two round carrot slices for eyes, an olive for a nose, and a curving celery stick made the smiling mouth. There was a tomato slice cut in half with each half placed on the side of the tuna mound, providing the ears. To finish it off, he added shredded lettuce on the top for hair.

I couldn't stop laughing. The manager who created the face walked in the room. He was so proud of his food art. He then declared, "Don't let anyone cut it until Arlo sees it."

Oh my God, I thought, if Arlo sees this, he may never eat tuna again. The coffee was a hotel-sized urn full of water alongside a jar of instant coffee and powdered milk. Next to those sat a Styrofoam cup. A coffee service that Arlo would dismiss as "plastic." Oh yes, it was just what I ordered for him.

I went next door to our hotel and the chef made me a fresh pot of coffee, a creamer full of cold half and half and a human-style coffee cup. I put the tuna table in the corner and discarded one carrot eye. I scooped a small helping of tuna and used some of the lettuce hair. There now! We had a nice little tuna fish salad, like he asked for. And the manager was so pleased with himself.

But then again, we had some of the most wonderful meals on the road. I remember we had the best, fried chicken ever in South Carolina. It was made by, and I quote the sweet lady herself: "You'll find this is the best little ole' fried chicken in the south, made by the littlest 'ole black lady in the south."

Me & Kay, one of Arlo's greatest fans—just ask Kay

This darling woman cooked the entire day in 90-degree heat in the basement kitchen located in the church next door to the venue. She served sweet potato pie, with her fabulous (and God, everything she made was fabulous) peach cobbler. She fed all of us. Arlo, the band, the crew ... and did it all herself.

When the show started and I sat alone in the dressing room, doing my paperwork, she came in and told me how to make her fried chicken! I've done it at home since. It's good—but of course, it's not as good as hers!

I'll share the recipe with you:

Rinse the chicken and pat dry.
Slide the chicken lightly through flour.
Dip chicken in sweetened, condensed canned milk.
Slide again through flour.
Deep fry.

Salt & pepper was added to the second batch of flour. The women who cook are the real "behind-the-scenes" people. Not the guys who set up the staging or who placed the lights, nor me, who did the paperwork and then was rewarded with gifts, from stuffed animals to monogrammed jackets. But those women who cooked homemade, wonderful food in such stifling heat and then cleaned up so you never knew they were there. They made our lives so much easier. I say thank you.

One of the hotels we were staying at happened to be a very ritzy place. We pulled into the underground garage of the hotel and were met by a butler dressed in a top hat, tails and white gloves. As we got off the bus in our cowboy boots and jeans he said, "Good evening Sir, lovely evening Ma'am!" They served tea in the afternoon at four o'clock with little teacakes. They served them again wearing the tails and gloves.

A folded white towel was draped over their arm as they took care of your every need. It was all so elegant and formal, as we all sat in our jeans. This was truly "tea and crumpets" in the afternoon.

If you came in with shopping bags, the elevator man would walk you to your room and either unlock your door or hold your bag for you while you opened the door. They were very classy and nice people.

Arlo backstage

The rooms were lovely. Each room had its own maid and monogrammed robe. The maid assigned to me came to my door somewhat stressed that she might be disturbing me. No, I told her, and asked what could I do for her?

She had an extra robe in a bag and said if I could get her an autograph from Mr. Guthrie then I could have the robe.

I replied, "Just knock on the door. He's not busy and he'll give you one."

"Oh no," she protested, "I'm not allowed!"

So I got her an autographed photo. And told her not to worry about any robe. I was glad to do it.

When I returned from the show that night, on my bed, along with the little chocolate was a nice note tucked into a packaged robe. There was also a robe for the T-shirt girl who was rooming with me.

"Please, my pleasure. We're so honored to have you here," she wrote, "that if there is anything we can do to make your stay more pleasant, just ring. And wear them in good health. (Signed) B.

"And P.S. The hotel allows us to do this with robes once per year. Again, B."

WE did a show near Cape Cod. They told me Joan Rivers played there the night before. It was a theatre in the round. They took out the last two rows of seats before she got there and moved people around so Joan would believe it was a sellout crowd. This was Joan's first live show since her husband Edgar killed himself and they wanted to protect her.

GALLIGHER

The following night after our show, Galligher was performing. After Arlo took the stage, I was in the dressing room doing paperwork. There was a knock on the door. I opened it to find Galligher standing there. He did not want to get there early and disrupt anything with Arlo's fans.

I gave him a glass of milk and he sat on the couch and we talked. He is one of the nicest and most handsome men. Galligher showed me a photo of his daughter that he always carries. I was so impressed with him. Galligher is a class act.

I mention these celebrities I met because I want to tell you what class acts these people are.

MARTIN SHEEN

We were doing a show in Las Vegas and I got a phone call at the hotel. It was Martin Sheen's secretary. Would it be possible for Martin and some of his people to hand out fliers about bomb testing in the desert? She wanted to know.

After a discussion and questions before an okay was given, she said if you have a minute stop and say hello. During intermission, after Arlo was seated with coffee, I went to the lobby. Off in a corner was Martin Sheen with five or six people handing out the fliers. I walked over and Mr. Sheen extended his hand with a warm welcome. He introduced me to everyone.

I asked if he would like to come back and say hello to Arlo?

"Oh, that would be real kind and I will if everyone can go," he said.

"Of course they can go," I replied.

We went backstage and Arlo was his usual gracious self, even though it was intermission and he was pressed for time.

Then we were ready for the second part of the show. I took the group back to the lobby and returned to get Arlo back on stage.

Yes, Martin Sheen is a class act.

JOHN PRINE

We did a lot of concerts across the country with John Prine. We would take turns opening the show. If we opened, then during intermission we would pack up and head right out for the next venue. And John would do the same, when he opened.

When John opened, I always watched his show. What a wonderful performer. He had a way of drawing you in, and he held you there, wanting more.

I remember once at Carnegie Hall when John did the second half. We stayed because we were all going to a great Indian restaurant afterwards. And there wasn't a show the next day—we would be going home.

Carnegie Hall has the strictest union of any venue. If you go over the eleven P.M. curfew deadline, there is a $1,000 fine per minute for going over.

John did not care about that. The veterans in the audience were his concern and he would just play and play. How they loved this guy. Yes, John Prine—another class act.

KRIS KRISTOFFERSON

Our sound checks were always at 5 P.M. so we had the day to do whatever we wanted. T-shirt Kathy and I headed down to the pool for an hour or so to lounge.

We were there for ten minutes when a fellow came along and sat next to me. I looked up and it was Kris Kristofferson.

No sooner did he sit down, when there were bodyguards all over the place. We said hello and started talking about the venue. We were playing tonight, and he was to play the following night.

He hadn't seen Arlo yet and was looking forward to spending some time together. The hour flew by and we had to leave. I said "I'll see you later," not really thinking I'd see him again.

The theatre darkened and Arlo went on stage. Fifteen minutes later, Kris snuck into the hall and took a seat in a quiet corner of the room. He came backstage after and spent some time with Arlo. He wouldn't interfere with Arlo's fans. Kris Kristofferson. He's another class act.

To me, the "behind the scenes" tells you everything. Arlo was a wonderful "behind the scenes" guy. He cared about the band members, the crew, and about everyone. I've seen him stand in the pouring rain signing photos or shirts or posters. If those fans stood out there waiting in the rain for him, he was thankful and would oblige. He'd stand right in the rain, along with them.

If we were at a restaurant in line and the manager found out Arlo was there, he'd want to bring him right in. Arlo would politely refuse. "Those people were there before me," he'd point out, "I cannot cut them off."

Arlo Guthrie—one class act.

PETE SEEGER

Now an entertainer we all know and love from old to young is Pete Seeger. How I remember fondly the times we spent with Pete, and all of his wonderful stories backstage.

The man is a wealth of information. Anything you want or need to know, Pete knew about, and if it took an hour to

tell, it would be the most interesting hour you could spenc.
Pete had an hypnotic storytelling abil:ty.

One time, I had to pick Pete up from the train station and
take him directly to the venue. We were supposed to meet
Arlo there and hoped to be on time. I hired a stretch limo to
pick me up and drive me to the depot.

When Pete saw me in the limo, he said, "Patricia, a taxi
would have been just fine. I don't neec this fancy car."

"I know, Pete," I protested, "but it's actually cheaper to
get a stretch limo than a cab out here!"

He winked at me in understanding at the irony and assured me it would be just fine. We made it to the show on
time and Pete and Arlo were wonderful, as they always were.

Dear Arlo — + Patricia
+ all — I woke up
at 5⁰⁰ + decided I
better catch a plane for
NYC. See you next
week in L.A. —J. Thanks
for handling all so well
yesterday — love Pete

his early morning swim in the hotel pool, then guitar, putting his money from the show inside leaving me a note he'd slipped under the door ...u ne headed for home and his wife, Toshi.

Pete Seeger—thee class act.

L ET me tell you about our trip to the Vietnam Veteran's Memorial in Washington, D.C. That trip is the most emotional visit you will ever make in your life. You make plans to go and everyone is excited to see the memorial. And then, you are standing in front of the wall. Your heart aches and you just sob. Your chest is pounding and it's hard to read the names through your tears.

You didn't know the men, but you can't stop reading their names. These men lost their lives to save yours and you are so overcome with emotion that when you do leave, that emotion stays with you for a long time.

We had a show to do in Washington, D.C. and I was thankful we did the show before we went to the memorial because the solemn mood lingered. All we can do is pray there never has to be another memorial like this.

"JUST Call Him Dr. Guthrie." That's what the headline said. Arlo was given an honorary doctorate from Siena College in Loudonville, New York in October 1981.

In May 1982, Arlo received the degree "Doctor of Humane Letters, *Honoris Causa*" from William P. Haas, President of North Adams State College.

He wrote this piece:

67

Arlo Guthrie

In the past fifteen years, you have become one of the best-known people in this land. Once it was the younger generation which admired you. Now, through your devotion to humane causes, you are celebrated by people of all ages and condition.

Your audience is held by the quality of your mind, while the world is stayed by the calm courage of your life.

With wit and love you draw us into the spacious chambers of your soul where you create something of value to humanity.

The words to your song, "I sit alone and hear the sparrow sing / No way of knowing what tomorrow brings / I leave my solitude upon its wing," convey the resonance of your spirit.

Gently, you have mastered the art of song and the art of living.

In recognition whereof, I confer upon you the degree Doctor of Humane Letters, *honoris causa*.

William P. Haas, President
North Adams State College
May 29, 1982

I N April, we pulled into the hotel parking lot. Being the first one—always—off the bus, I went into the lobby to start the paperwork needed for our stay.

I did the rooming lists for each one of us. I got our room keys, time sheets and restaurant locations nearest the hotel. As it was April 12, my birthday, I saw all the flower bouquets on the counter and I jokingly said to the receptionist, "Oh, which one is mine?"

She laughed and replied, "Oh honey! Take your pick!"

As I'm signing in, the florists came in with a beautiful basket. And he announced, "Patricia Lampro—has she arrived?"

I took the card, read it, and I burst into tears. My family, including our dog Susie sent such beautiful flowers. Then just as I'm sobbing, I turned and behind me stood Arlo, the band, and the driver all applauding and singing "Happy Birthday to you!"

Arlo said, "Trish, when you finish here, meet me in the restaurant."

I must have looked a mess—I was crying and couldn't even talk. I gave everybody room keys and papers and then left to meet Arlo.

"Let's have a sandwich and coffee," he offered, and he called our waiter over.

As I reached to get a Kleenex from my purse, Arlo placed a box in front of me. "Happy Birthday, Trish—you can open it now if you like." I took off the lid to find a red watch. It was beautiful and I cried all over again. Arlo laughed and said, "Trish, it's okay."

As we traveled around the country, we did our share of sightseeing. Every time we left a hotel, the desk clerk would ask where we were going next. Then comes the day we're all excited about because it's the next leg of our trip.

I was at the counter checking out and waiting to hear the inevitable question, "Where are you going next?"

My answer was all ready—"We're going to Graceland! Graceland!"

But guess what? This guy never asked! We went to Graceland. We had a private tour and found it to be just the way we heard about and pictured. Afterward, we went to the gift shop and there in Elvis' gift shop, people were surrounding Arlo for his autograph.

One hotel we stopped at while on tour in Florida left me forever—always checking, very thoroughly—every bed I slept in or even sat on. When we arrived at any hotel as I've said, I was the first off the bus and into the lobby. I'd get the keys while checking off a rooming list I had made, and had also sent ahead to every hotel. The arrival time and instructions were given well in advance. Bus parking as well as finding local restaurants was among my requirements, along with securing the rooms, to be accessible upon arrival.

(Well, I'm told) the rooms wouldn't be ready for another hour. This would not do, and I let them know it. I was not the least bit happy. We needed those rooms—now.

I asked for the manager.

"Oh sorry," said the desk attendant, "no need for the manager!" And all of a sudden they found a block of rooms for us. So we do keys, add numbers to each rooming list and then the crew is behind me with their hands out, waiting.

After I get my luggage and go to my room, I change my clothes for the show. I was rooming with Gretchen and we were both getting ready. Everything seems fine, it's a lovely room.

We do sound check and have dinner and then Arlo does a wonderful concert. At midnight, we headed back to the hotel. We were all tired and a nice, hot shower followed by a good night's sleep is just what the doctor ordered.

We are so ready! I unlocked our door, turned the light switch on and Gretchen and I stepped into our room. I put my briefcase on the desk and turned to sit on my bed.

T-shirt Gretchen on our day off (I would never do this!)

And there in the middle of the bedspread lay not the little nighttime candies they place on your pillow, but a cluster of five dead cockroaches in a little pile—just waiting for me and my reaction.

Bob, Terry, Flo, Me, Arlo, Kathy and David

And did I ever have a reaction. I'm sure if the crew from the front desk hadn't been listening outside of my door, they could hear me in the lobby anyway. I made my way from the third floor in record time. I announced loudly, "Now I will see the manager!"

He came out of his office and I took him up to the room. When he saw the dead bugs and heard the check-in story, he got us a key to a lovely suite. He apologized profusely, telling me the suite would be a gift as well as breakfast for me and whoever joined my table. He didn't know, but on occasion, all of us would sit together. And I made sure that all of us would sit together in the morning!

I'm not vindictive, but those guys at the front desk were in for a lot of trouble and I was really looking forward to their just rewards.

WHEN you're in the office as secretary, you make doctor appointments, schedule interviews, pay the help, read contracts, pay bills, make airport trips—both drop offs and pick ups. You deliver paperwork to lawyers and call plumbers and other repairmen. You arrange meetings, attend meetings, and type up the reports. All of the filing is done at your convenience. You make travel plans, booking flights and reserving hotels.

Add all of the social events and a few more duties in the office and before you know it, the day is over. And all of this is done at your own pace.

But when you're on the road, there's no such thing as "your own pace." Timing is everything. Wake up calls, bus loading, check-ins, checkouts, sound checks, and then dinner, menus, intermissions, dressing rooms, reporters, settling concert fees, and then it's SHOW TIME! Everything is done at a specific time.

Laundry has to be done, per diem paid, phone calls to Harold squeezed in, interviews, bank transactions, and of course—shopping and sight seeing. A lot of times, our days off would turn out to be travel days. But it all gets done. And the show goes on. We all travel well together.

Then all of a sudden, the tour is over. We go back home, spend time with our families and regroup. After a few weeks at home, we'd start the bookings for the next tour. It will be three months on the road, living out of a suitcase. Everyone does their part and we're all fresh and rested and ready to roll!

BUT while we were home, Arlo got himself a tractor and loved to be outside doing things around the farm. He'd be pulling up tree stumps and putting in fence posts.

If he was working in the upper fields, Jackie would go up with a picnic lunch and they'd spend an hour talking about the plans they had to add a driveway here or there so the bus could make one run right around the building. In the winter when he was home, he'd plow the driveway and he absolutely loved snowstorms. The snow banks were extremely high and the kids had a lot of fun using them as sliding hills.

MY son Jimmy was going to be married and all the preparations were in place. The big event was to take place at our mother church, which is just ten minutes away.

Arlo was home on a break so he and Jackie came to the wedding. After the service, Arlo went home and because he was so moved by the day, wrote a song titled—appropriately enough—"The Wedding Song." When the song was recorded, my son-in-law, Pete Adams is featured playing pedal steel:

WEDDING SONG

Poor Adam alone in Eden
Taking off his shoes
Tired from running around all morning
From his animal interviews
He awoke with a hand on his brow
Asking, Who are you?
They spent the rest of their lives together
Making their debuts dressed in leaves and wearing blues

Some say one thing, some say two
Ain't much about it anyone can do
Keep on walking 'til my soles wear through
Wearing away my shoes
Evening comes and the sky turns red
Clouds of colors cover up our heads
Ain't it something just to lie here in bed
Just me and you

Oh Mary, wrapped up in glory
What are you going to tell your groom?
How's he going to feel on the day of your wedding?
What will your friends assume?
Oh, but Joseph and Mary were married
The angels carried the news
What the Lord has joined together

The world must not undo

There's a wedding down at the church this morning
Let's go wish them well
It's a beautiful day for getting married
I hope the weather lasts as well
It's been years since we've been married
I know we paid some dues
Now ain't it something just to lie here together
Just me and you outlasting the blues

Arlo at Alleluia House

A RLO did a concert to benefit the exceptional children and adults of Jericho. He spent time with the children and was shown everything that went on at Jericho. Father Robert Wagner devoted his life to Alleluia House and aiding the retarded. Father Wagner had the help of six nuns, his secretary, and 300 to 400 volunteer workers. They serve more than 1,000 retarded people all over Western Massachusetts.

Arlo was very proud to take an active part in Alleluia House. And he is very proud of the children there. We are all children of God. To donate to Jericho you can write:

Jericho c/o Alleluia House
35 Northampton Street
Holyoke, MA 01049

ON a trip to California, we had a day off and Arlo said if we wanted, we would layover spending the day in Las Vegas and we could gamble and play all we wanted. We were all in agreement. This ought to be a lot of fun.

I got everyone the keys and information and went back out to the bus to get my suitcase. The driver had already moved the bus, not waiting for me to get my things when everyone else had. I walked up to the bus, now idling at a distance. I followed him as he moved the bus a little at a time. The bay to the bus was open—but he kept moving. So I kept following. All of a sudden, he stopped and I caught up with him. It is illegal to drive with the bay open.

I tapped on the door and told him I was going to take my suitcase from the bay. Just as I reached in to get my bag, he moved the bus—so I jumped back.

He stopped. I tried to reach in again, but he moved the bus again. He could see me in the mirror, because I could see him. He was trying to run me over.

I didn't show any emotion. I simply said, "Play your games," and walked back to the hotel, steamed. I went to my

room with my head held high but when I got there, I was
shaking and I sat down and started to cry. But he never knew
he got to me, and I never told Arlo about that incident.

There had been a discrepancy with that driver which I
had discovered earlier, but I handled it my way, and correct-
ed the issue discreetly. Regardless, he didn't like that he had
been found out. But because I had resolved to maintain my
cool, the bus incident blew over.

But I never let my guard down again.

I learned the ropes as a road manager from Bruce Clapper. "B.C." took over as Arlo's road manager after John Pilla.
Bruce knew the business inside and out, along with Gary Fish,
another of our favorites and the best of John Prine's manag-
ers—firm, understanding, knowledgeable and always caring.

B.C. let me tag along behind him as I watched him
check us into hotels, give out keys and room lists, restaurant
lists, departure times and announce (only once) show times.
I listened to him set up interviews for TV and radio and
newspapers; check us out of hotels, arrange parking, check
dressing rooms, send money to Harold in New York, and
keep everyone in line—then enter all this info into books.
These are some (there's more) road manager responsibili-
ties, mostly at night, after everyone else is asleep. And I was
in line to take it all on.

Bruce went on to run his own tour bus company, and then
settled in doing sound for many singers. He's now back doing
sound for Arlo.

My son Jody was back on the road touring with Arlo this
past winter, as well as Abe Guthrie and Bobby Sweet and Terry a la Berry and The Burns Sisters. Abe and Jody room together and are a perfect match with the same birthdays! Both
are "Aries", both born on April 1st, to be exact.

The new road manager was nicknamed "Killer" by Arlo; he usually names everyone (that's Carrie to her family). She's great, I love her and they all love her. Killer's one of the best in the business. Her personality is wonderful and she's so cute—go get 'em, Killer!

And then there's Terry! I must tell you about Terry a la Berry, friend, drummer, entertainer, comedian and charmer. Terry can light up a room and be the most entertaining in that room—always with grace and charm.

Danny Velika and Terry were the best of friends. They often golfed together, whether at home or on the road. One time, when we were in Texas, they played 18 holes at Willie Nelson's golf course. They ended up with tee's with Willie's name on them, which Dan said they treasured.

Terry could make a tough situation easy and funny. Only when Danny died suddenly did Terry have a hard time. I'm

After a day of fishing

sure he misses his dear friend terribly. On this past winter's tour, Terry roomed with Bobby Sweet—also among the nicest guys, as well a talented singer-songwriter and musician.

Ray and me

THE Guthrie children have grown up now with families of their own, and they all have followed in the their father's and grandfather Woody's footsteps by being involved with music. Abe plays keyboard like he was born holding it in his hands and is also a solid sound engineer. Sarah Lee plays guitar, writes music, sings and performs widely with her husband Johnny Irion. Cathyaliza plays mandolin and sings with Amy Nelson, Willie Nelson's daughter. Annie Hayes is also a singer-songwriter with rich vocals, and she and Cathy together now handle Arlo's business end. The three girls have performed together as "The G Babes."

Billie's daughter at Willie Nelson show with my Kathy, Willie, Terry and me

Abe's son, Krishna Guthrie is a young, budding singer-songwriter and guitarist, and Sarah's daughter, Olivia Irion pops on stage during her parents' shows so I believe the Guthrie music will continue for many generations to come.

So life goes on. I lost my husband Frannie and my Mother five weeks apart. I retired. I tried new things. I did new things.

Then I met a man who is so wonderful and we are so very compatible. He's the love of my life. We are enjoying our lives together. We winter in Florida and spend our summers in Massachusetts. We enjoy my children and grandchildren.

We play golf and enjoy all the daily pleasures life has to offer two people in their later years. And in the meantime, I have such great memories of me and Arlo. It was always personal.

POSTSCRIPT

As this book was written and sent to print, my sister Billie had her surgery and she died on the operating table on August 2, 2005, with her four children and our sister Jeanne at her side. I thank Jeanne and her husband Johnny with all my heart, for always being there. Johnny with his sense of humor and Jeanne as his straight man are priceless. Even though they did so much for Billie and saw so much of her pain, they kept us all going through those tough times with their laughter. I love you guys.

One of my sister Billie's favorite photos—meeting the Smothers Brothers. We're backstage at her first concert (me, Tommy, Billie, Dickie).